THE LAST SACRED PLACE

IN NORTH AMERICA

Also by Stephen Haven

Dust and Bread
(poetry, 2008)

The River Lock: One Boy's Life Along the Mohawk
(memoir, 2008)

The Enemy in Defensive Positions: Poems from China
(editor and co-translator, 2008)

The Long Silence of the Mohawk Carpet Smokestacks
(poetry, 2004)

And What Rough Beast: Poems at the End of the Century
(co-editor, 1999)

Scarecrow Poetry: The Muse in Post-Middle Age
(co-editor, 1994)

The Poetry of W.D. Snodgrass: Everything Human
(editor, 1993)

THE LAST SACRED PLACE

IN NORTH AMERICA

POEMS

Stephen Haven

newamericanpress

Milwaukee, Wisconsin • Urbana, Illinois

n e w   a m e r i c a n   p r e s s

www.NewAmericanPress.com

Printed in the United States of America

ISBN 978-0-9849439-0-6

Cover photo © 2010 by Aleksandra Bogdanova
Book design by David Bowen

For ordering information, please contact:

Ingram Book Group
One Ingram Blvd.
La Vergne, TN 37086
(800) 937-8000
orders@ingrambook.com

For My Mother,

The Gift of Her Laughter,

Sallie Harcourt Haven

1931-2008

CONTENTS

I

II

III

I

SPLASHDOWN: APOLLO 13

Though they failed to show it on the evening news
The taut sail of the *Rachel* leaned to gather
The *Odyssey*'s tossed crew. In the corked bottle

Of the command module, the folded message of astronauts
Like something about to bloom.
Small explosives popped the hatch, then out

Of some vast place they were themselves again,
Bobbing in rubber rafts, waiting for their restoration
To women, children, though now they carried with them

The blue planet shot from the moon,
Floating like a hologram, or some glassed jewel.
They weighed things black and blue,

The sheer stretch of where they were delivered
From and to, now a horizon
That would not keep still, the small company of men

More at home with each other now
In a blank expanse that cupped and cradled them.
Yes, it was the *Rachel*, and the web

Of that inhuman view, the Earth's crescent
Rising from behind the moon, and clear in the ear,
The whole ride home, something softer,

•

Darker than any dissonance,
Calling from an absence of children:
Joseph long gone by now, Benjamin missing,

And their long progeny dreaming of milk and honey
In the desert of our own century. *O Egypt, O exile,*
O voice from the fire of our own mast tops, O Ariel,

Speak to us again, beyond the last candle,
Of the New World naked, of the West hanging
Somewhere above us, always in the balance,

The planet riding the bronco
Of Hubble's peephole, and rising with each swell,
Ishmael hugging the lifeboat of his coffin,

The light so barren it was only before imagined,
The spread skirt of a ship approaching,
Abraham, Hagar, even Sarah waiting

In the wings of a wound that might heal them....
The *Rachel* tacked to gather them,
Then helicopters dropped their spun strands,

Lifted them into a world they once knew.
In the understory of that new aerial view
A still, small voice absent of its womb.

ROOM IN A ROOM

Headlands Center for the Arts
Fort Barry, Sausalito, California

Afternoons you make the trek to pivot
In the old turrets and wave hello
To the razors and chains of abandoned missile silos,

One guard still luminous beside his trap door,
Signaling from his Hawk Tower.
Jeffers haunts you too, though this is your own

Bare-bone studio, where Navy officers once stared out
A World War II window: J. Daniels, Chesterfields
And the radar's nervous tick, the still world

About to bloom, eternity the time it took
To sight a no show, first Japanese Zeroes.
A groundless, well-founded fear,

Bunkered in these hills, till in the plush
Of each long night Light Wardens wander still,
Extinguish every spark. The entire

Thousand mile coastline goes dark.
Then pelicans like pterodactyls
In first light to the sea, the dunes beneath you,

•

Black rock once spewed from a volcano.
Your mind cannot contain it, not your small digit,
One chair, one desk, nothing to distract

But this screen, this wireless, this one-lane pull
Of a tunnel beyond which the handkerchiefs
Of yachts drift. Inside this Chinese box,

Not even Mexico can gather the orphans of her lost children
As they lift to the view of the crescent blue planet
Shot from the moon. Drifting, drifting

In their module, the crippled Apollo 13 crew
Deep in shadow: When the sea finally rocks them,
The sun fits like a baseball in the mitt of Arcturus.

A priest lifts a chalice just beyond the tongue tip.
A dead star drifts to the mind that regards it,
Its strange light scarring the film of who we are.

You pull it up from where you sit, left click:
There on your screen your cursor flicks
Like a water whisk in the black till.

As you watch the Earth takes off, finally,
Its skull cap made of ice entirely. No north,
No cardinal points. Once, at the urging

•

Of your five-year-old, your entire family
Beached clothes by the side of the road.
Your gonads shrunk to walnuts:

That's about the size of 'em, your wife said.
But now, beneath you, just past noon,
Already the children gather in a quilt of mothers,

Digging for China, throwing to the break
As always and ever and never again
Pebbles and seashells and fistfuls of sand.

SHELTER

First there was light at the Trinity test site, then a wind
Of Biblical hubris that peeled back skin, flashed
The teeth of our own skeletons. We felt at once
Amazed, diminished and afraid, awe for the cradle
Of some new revelation, our birth stars cupped in its crater.
We became the authors of our own destiny and power,
Self-made gods for whom there was only Truman
To play the wise man, wiping on his shirt sleeves
The blood from Oppy's hands, some small-town faith
Squaring itself with this new spigot, with the common man
Who worshiped this new sun like some ancient
Coin-eyed Egyptian. We built new backyard temples,
New mausoleums, stocked with food, with ammo
For the underworld, and waited for good reason
To bury ourselves in dirt and shoot our fellow citizens.

MINUTE MAN

God-like phallus of our day, it is time you stood for something,
Time you explained. We have lived within the omnipresence
Of your reign. Fountain of peace and Armageddon, all-powerful,
Tyrannical, merciful, you have not yet dispatched us in a flash
From your subterranean burrows, or from low orbit
Shot down at us, fish in a barrel. No one witnessed you,
Invisible, hovering over the billboards of our age,
And yet we think you are there just the same,
Like Yahweh sparing Nineveh for some light reason
While Jonah sulks in the shelter of the Yggdrasil tree
Damned if he'll say a word because the world won't burn
As always it has not burned. Jealous of justice, God-stuffed,
Cracked by his own silence, damned if he'll play the fool,
A mongerer of fear but sure in his own knowledge,
He sits beneath the union of Earth, history, and heaven,
Bereaved by his own comfort, the tree rotting itself half-way
To hell, the upper branches Orion's belt. We wait in his image,
Alive, still born, not quite free, off in the shade somewhere
Where there is no sign, in the silent power of the periphery.

M.A.D.

What would you say, I asked my children, if you found
I was secreting away grenades, M-16s, chemical fertilizer,
Never let you see the attic TNT, explosives of all sizes,
Shapes and colors, enough to take down ourselves,
Our neighbors, if someone so much thought
To steal your bicycles, or looked at your mother wrong,
Or mowed across our line, where there is no fence
Except the one in my mind, the best defense
Always a good suicide, as long as it takes
Half the world besides, the origin of that violence
A love that finds its resonance only in the tribe?

What if I offered you only this thread of history
And a spool from the attic on which to wind it
And asked you to fuse it into the hems
Of the jackets of your children, this prize,
Love fortified, and not like Magda Goebbels'
Sweet cyanide, more like the Romans,
More like samurai, something of honor in it,
More like the Palestinian who crosses the border
With her wires, to help the wounded cur
Of a dead dog die?

MONOLITH

Still the poets wrote of their mothers, their fathers,
Of their favorite rust-red houses in the deepest recesses
Of loved cul-de-sacs. They scraped skateboards off ramps.
In their gray hour they plumbed the funeral pyre
Of blossoms they discovered endlessly exorcising
And reinventing themselves, the plumb or level line,
Some vantage point, some holocaust of mind
Casting colors like a film projector, how such things
Never gained a foothold in nature, so why ever
In poetry and architecture, new figures, new orders
Coined for each new day, each one fully temporary,
Absolute and necessary, of nature and man-made,
While in the pup tent of the central cortex,
In the form of Kubrick's black monolith,
There was no chatter and this time no laughter.
Though something shattered nothing broke.
From their old chairs the poets took note,
From the language of love and dust looked up
And cupped their spent fathers, the lovely interior
Made by their mothers, and the curve of each year's flowers.

TALISMAN

The Funeral Director said *Turn at the Purple Gorilla.*
His suit was one size too big, the gorilla
The only landmark he offered. *You can't miss it.*

We thought he referred to a lounge of some kind
And kept our eyes sharp for the sign.
Good, we thought, afterward we might need a drink.

Some thirty miles off the West Virginia border,
Half-way to another state of mind,
We knew we missed the mark.

The FD helped us when we celled back in
And found our way again, and then we saw them,
A polka-dotted giraffe, a pink and yellow zebra,

Monkeys of all sizes, a regular ceramic zoo
On the highway's side, and the tell-tale gorilla,
Our talisman, our ringmaster.

We knew we had arrived when we drew past
That indigenous ark into the more
Dirt than gravel drive, the tight rope of a plank

Bending toward a puddle as we crossed from lot
To porch. *Forgive our Progress*, the FD said,
Thin as the smoke from his Lucky Strike.

•

My brother and our wives closed in,
Held hands, the rest of the family outside
In my father's van. They waited beside

The dumpster, its mouth open like a shovel.
Behind the window we could see him,
Wrapped in his final dignity.

My mother had dressed him in his last vestments,
An old maroon pair of pajamas, white robe,
Slippers we picked up in some Blue Light Special.

The odds were with him this time as he maintained
Amidst the chaos some deep inner peace.
When the FD's assistant closed him up

And hit him twice in the face, my father never flinched.
Then they lifted the ossuary of his cardboard coffin.
Then the floodwaters of the oven took him.

I did not forgive them, neither did I blame
The Appalachian edge of where I live.
This was America, after all, this was Boston,

New York City, Omaha.... Anywhere
My father ever lived, the unornamented dead
Kept their own counsel as these purple fists,

Half hidden in a continent of grass,
Marked in the service of their salute
Our errand into the wilderness....

STOLE

In the moment my father died, we did not want to spend
Another dollar for the twenty-four hours
He would no longer be living
In the Willow Haven full-care facility.

We lobbied the nurses to credit the last moment
He breathed among us. It was four-thirty A.M.,
April 26, 2007. Who in their right mind
Would call that a day? Maybe if we had him out

By dawn, someone said.
When she said that, my mother directed me
To lift a La-Z-Boy into our old van.
Sometimes the yarmulke of the human hand

Is all we need to press us back to earth again.
Don't worry, my brother said,
Strange things might happen
In this exact moment. My father was not

A wealthy man. We gathered all
His stray accoutrements—toothbrush, razor,
A lifetime of reading bound up
In his last book, Robinson's *Gilead*....

•

He lay there in that precise moment
While the nurses, lovely women all,
Stripped and washed him, then set out
A fresh pair of pajamas. My mother cried,

Kissed him on the forehead. Socks or no socks,
Someone asked? In the economics
Of that exact moment, we ordered only
A cardboard coffin, everything he ever wanted.

Then they swung him in his last sheet,
Flat on a gurney, a sail-wrapped sailor
Rolling toward the deep.
Some man in jeans and a colored BVD

Steered him down the hallway.
He hoped it was okay
With my brother and me, mud on his
Cherokee SUV…. I wanted to stay

A long while in the brake lights' glow
But somewhere in an absence
Of underwriters and sacraments
One last time my father put on his stole.

Too young to receive
A child bared his head.
Then all the universe weighed in
For the altered touch of the priest.

BLOOD BLESSING

Your oxygen line trailed after the weekends
I drove down to visit a day or two:
In the helmet of each breath,

In your eighty-year-old bubble,
We swung through our New York years
An ax for kindling and shoveled snow.

I still find you there in black and white,
A silence my children find strange,
The absent tick of it converted to VHS:

Young and limber, smoking your pipe again
In some bare-wood Canadian cabin.
Minus a sound track, you still read

To my brothers, my sister, and me
(Spent sprinter, deep sea diver),
The spine of it clear on the screen:

Moby Dick! Not one of us yet seven!
There was a dog that drawn summer
So white they called him Caspar, paws raw

From the hot sand. And a clown I remember
Riding the bronco of a motorboat's bow.
When he fell, when he surfaced on the beach,

•

We could see the shock of blood and genitals
Through the shred of his false smile
And pink pantaloons. We picked

Blackberries in the hills
And ate them as quickly as they filled
Our gray buckets. Okay, Okay, I accept now

Everything you ever brought to me,
Failed and broken, pregnant with new meaning,
Beauty and bearing, literature and liturgy,

Not as a man but as a man might be,
Fallen, falling into possibility.
In our gray upstate New York three-story

You'd read away whole Sunday afternoons
Stopping only for cocktails at five
Or to feed a rip-roaring fire.

"You're headed to a better place,"
Your neighbor, unschooled in you,
Made the faux pas to offer:

"There's a blessing in this somewhere...."
"Don't ever make the mistake
Of preaching to a preacher," you shot back,

•

One month left, your skepticism riding
In the same seat as your belief.
Almost without complaint those weeks

You accepted every pill and still poured through
A book that haunts the sign
For Mt. Gilead, Ohio. When you were done,

You started over again, then could not lift
Even the weight of that last paperback.
I called on Robinson, I called on Ames,

My brother, my father, my clergyman,
And read to you once while you slept
That being blessed meant being bloodied,

"…that is true etymologically in English
But not in Greek or Hebrew."
A deep, familial voice filled the room:

"Of the liver," you said, "of the good color
In your cheeks. That's what they once thought
Before the Renaissance."

LAST WORDS

Suddenly she loved the floral print
Of the wallpaper and thought how strange
It was: Till now she hadn't noticed it.
She had been asleep six days or more.
"What's the big deal, what?" she said. "Let's let
A little light in here," I said, and drew
The curtains back. She laughed and laughed.
"You're so funny," she said, and in that moment
Of laughter I saw for the first time teeth
Too large for a head. "What's the big deal?"
"You need to swallow," I said, "if you're going
To get well again." The RN mixed
Vanilla in. I heard someone singing
About sugar and medicine. "That tastes
Wonderful," my mother said, a stethoscope
At her throat to measure the full power
Of a swallow. "You're so sweet," she said,
While the nurse worked and my mother
Dripped and seeped. I will remember
For a long, long time, *"More pudding,"*
My mother said. For a moment I thought
Yellow is the color of love, so Doctor
Williams says. Her eyes were full of it,
Her skin soaked in it. Then pain reconnoitered
Her again. For two whole days I played
Sacred hymns, Numbers 6:24-26
On her stereo, over and over again.

THE LAST SACRED PLACE IN NORTH AMERICA

Outside the Rothko Chapel, in Houston, Texas,
Short of its jagged tip,
Newman's *Broken Obelisk*
Murmurs in the COR-TEN polish of its lift
Of perfection or something like it
Then cracks to spill seeds of air,
An unrequited plumb of love,
A broken arrow that never hummed
From the taut bow much less
Missed the mark. *That's how the light*
Gets in, a crack in everything....
So with this King (MLK)
When the final word was broken....

Then flush inside the building, if only
You listen, the thrum of a dark hush
As if you could hear Space's own
B flat drone. Rhapsody in Black
Whistler might have called it
But this is Rothko, this the late song
Of our own diminuendo
As it goes down now, not yet
To nothing, *piano, pianissimo,*
As if we were ourselves
Only our own echo,
The lyrics spent, the voice of the singer
Distantly near: You cannot say

•

Where the tonic lies, whether in some
Cure of ground or sky, midnight's monolith
Fletching at each cardinal the susurrus quiver
Of these dark panels. Your own caesurae,
Your own circumference,
Is the shell of a missing animal.
You pull it tight around you like a cloak,
This riff that keeps on breathing
Through flaws, through fissures,
Pole of the thin
Man out on a wire. It teeters, pivots on
The dominant. Cup one ear.
You can almost hear.

EXIT THE KING

Tonight you're watching TNT: The old World Champs
Going down, losing it in a public way,
And the young Turks jeering from the sideline
Of the new reign. No slam dunk, not even when you're
Future Hall of Fame. You think of Sondheim
At the top of his game, Little Red Cap
Now strictly old hat, trumping even old Eugen once,

Though now Geoffrey Rush has brought him back again.
Exit the King and then what enters in?
A little thunder, a little rain, long laughter, long silence,
Center stage. You go away for a few
Early April days, and there it is as you drive up
The night's journey from the plane:
The same tree blooms, a ghost of its formal self,

The loss of the new that keeps right on renewing itself
Right at the edge of where you mow.
Some days your neighbor lets you know, you cross
At your own peril. Firing on all cylinders,
Beyond months of snow, you pull up,
Pause before you hit the remote:
The night flames, the one white tree you own.

II

FU HAN AT THE NUTS CAFÉ, CHONGQING, CHINA, APRIL 9, 2011

Then it begins, "some famous Beijing band,"
Her bleached flop jelly fishing as she hops on stage,
Flings her spiral-lensed, psychedelic shades,
And then her wings, some feathered shawl,
Bird-like even when she sheds them,
Her long, graceful arms. She must weigh all
Of ninety pounds, singing of the man on the moon,
Or K-I-L-L-*L-L-L*, K-I-*SSS*, boogying
Like the best of them. Some stubborn strain
Where in a few words, deep in some slumber,
The old, grizzled monolith of history stirs,
The lead guitar a little stiff, the bass-line driving
A Cadillac straight from Flint, then arcing out
Some exit nowhere near Liverpool or Haight-Ash.
Five black Chinese swans on a man-made pond,
Willows and bamboo all the way around
Somewhere in the song. With one arm lifted high,
Hand arced inward, she says *I am, I am, I am!*
To which I add, *Says the Lamb!* Then she offers

The mic to her admirers. Whatever song they're singing
It's not Tiananmen, the bass line digging in again,
Fu Han whirlin and girlin it, till I wonder if this
Is what the Blue Note was, some passion you could
Never quite measure, everything not yet thirty
Chanting in a bar, while the years,

Thousands of them here, line up and bear
Only one Fu Han. I lean toward some girl
Crushed against me, *"Tamen jiao shenme mingzi?"*
"Queen Sea Big Shark," she says it in Chinese.
"Speak slowly, please...." She hands me their card:
Then all night long, fifteen flights above Chongqing,
I can hear, beneath me, all of North America
Singing in some inner sanctum of the '90s,
Lord, I have loved thy lowly, the poor of thy house....
Stories beneath her laugh, Fu Han whispers back,
Fuck that! The Earth, some stranger, seen
From afar, everything blue, our old turntable
Cranking some old scratched tune.

PING PONG PARK, CHONGQING, CHINA, MARCH 27, 2011

The sun shines nowhere here. Gray most days. Sullen spring
Riffs on the bass. The lead guitar's industrial haze.
Now, everywhere in the parks no one lectures
From outdoor sound systems about politics, the art
Of maintaining Left Thinking. Still, loud speakers
Line the walks: A pop star croons, nothing close to rock,
About love and beauty, surely. If I could understand her
I'd sing along with her false note, as I do so often
When I am home, mouthing Otis Redding,
Sitting on the dock of the bay, when I do not know

The relevance to me, really, why nothing pulls
Like the sun, the tides, the Georgia he's left behind,
Ships rolling in, rolling away again. In my bones
I know a man that alive will never die,
Dead when he was twenty-six years old.
Sure, I feel a lift this far from home.
I stop to photograph a ping pong court,
Ask in pidgin Mandarin, "No problem? No problem?"
"Hello! Hello!" A woman ten years my senior
Offers up her paddle. That I can say

At least something in her own lilt delights her.
She gives me the thumbs up when I return
A deep shot. Eight ping pong tables,
Green and still as aircraft carriers

From which small things take flight.
They used to play with a line of bricks for nets,
Errant shots ricocheting until the balls cracked.
Prosperity's a racket privileging the parks,
Tennis and badminton courts. The old man,
My partner, shows me how to hold

The paddle gripped in a vertical rather than
A horizontal fist. "I am not good," I say,
"My son is good. I do not know," and hold the handle
As he showed me, "My son knows." "Very good,"
He says to me: "Good," I say, then he spins
Some ninety miles per hour phrase. "New York,
New York," I say, a place they seem to know,
Though I am from Ohio now. In the blossoms
Of a few trees spring nudges through the haze.
A red dog on a blue tree. A blue dog

On a red tree, a green dog on a yellow tree.
"Xiexie, xiexie!," I say, *"Zaijian la!"*
"Goodbye, goodbye," they call after me.
I feel my way back to Campus B,
Chongqing University, some nasal soprano
Following me as I walk: *No problem, No problem,*
Singing of the world's fat heart.

THREE POEMS BY MANG KE

tr. Stephen Haven and Wang Shouyi

People Age Even After Death

From the bodies of the dead
White hair grows
People age even after death

Nightmares haunt them in the grave
Startle them awake
They open their eyes and see

Another day is hatched
Pecking for food in the fields

Day hears its own footsteps
The laughter, the sorrow
Of its own body, recalls

In its heart, though its brain
Is empty, all the rotting corpses

The day sings of them
And of its own lover
It holds her face steady
With its two hands

•

Then it puts her back
Cautiously in the grass,
The sexy drag of her body

The day may wait for sunshine
But finally, an old straw mattress,
The wind blows it away

The day waits for dusk
When it will hide from you
As if in fear of the savagery
Of a wild beast

But at night, at night, it is so tender
Released, you can pull it wordless
Into your arms
Play with it as you like

Maybe it will lie down on the spot
Exhausted, its eyes closed
Listening to the roar of the fighting
Of heavenly beasts

Day may worry, on that one night
The heavens might open, blood rain down

It may stand up moaning
At the face of the dead,
A woman whose eyes stare and stare

•

It may hope, may wish itself
Alive forever, not a hunted animal

Not roasted in the fire
Not swallowed
Though the pain is still unbearable

From the bodies of the dead
White hair grows
Even after death, they age and age

In the Street

I can't be sure of my age today:
Maybe I am only ten years old.
But I know my mind, my mind
Thinks of filthy things.
Today, on the street,
I step hard on the shadow of a girl.
A baby totters in the gutter,
Then falls asleep, his hip cupped
By someone I don't know.
An old man, not far from me,
Grabs some nastiness from the ground.
I don't know. No one notices.
Kids piss in the street,
Their bellies open to the sun.
Suddenly, a dog of all things

41

Scampers by. I run too. Nobody knows
Who retched his dinner in the street.
I look away. Suddenly,
A woman, a pair of bedroom eyes
Nails me, balloons like the fat man
Who also stares at me. I hardly know
Why they accost me in this way.
What does that fat man have in mind?
Then someone slaps a cat—
Who knows what for? It runs off
Whimpering to one retarded man,
The mad whining to the mad.
I think: why not jump up and scratch
Someone's face, cat? The idiot gapes.
Okay, run off! Cat, I wish you
No good end. Then high up
On a building, some girl's ugly face
Pokes out an open window.
I say, *Hey there!,* teasing her
To the point of fear. Such a serious girl!
Then a woman, her face like a siren,
Rushes away. Close behind
The cussing of her man,
All to the lewd amusement of the crowd.
One guy spits, hits the picture
Of a woman on the wall behind him.
Then some bum, so blind he scours
The street with his feet,
Bumps into me. In favor of food
The crowd scatters off, the richest

To restaurants. Some sleek-haired guy
Heads for the shitter,
Running, unbuckling on the way.
Even the sun escapes in a hurry
As if it had a home.
Then it's darker. I wander.
In the street, my silence. My hunger.

You, Dead Day

Once I walked in this same street with you
Saw you with open eyes
Dead in the street
I felt the earth suddenly pulled
Out from under our feet
The stickiness of that void
Although I yelled, although I tried
The sorrow of escape—no use
I sank down and down
Worrying in the last moment
Of the smothered future

THE BUTTERFLY AND THE FLOWERS

—Su-Shih, sung to the tune of "Die Lian Hua"
tr. Stephen Haven and Wang Shouyi

Flowers, pale, dry, fallen all around,
Tiny light-green apricots.

Swallows flying high and low,
Green water easing through scattered homes.

The sponge-like catkins in the willow
Thin, thinner in the wind.

No corner in this whole world
Lacks the grace of this sweet grass.

Inside the locked wall, in the lift
Of a swing, the laughter of one woman.

Outside a man, gun shy, walking beneath
The flash of his own life, her momentary peak.

He has no tongue to stir the pain,
Her silence absolute in the final downswing.

THE LAST TRAIN BY

You draw close in the vacuum of its pass,
A railroad defunct for ages, now,
And the still *whoosh* of a train just past.
Then in the distance, your eye picks out
Some rusted denouement, the endgame
Of the last car's flash that never
Quite disappears and is always fading fast.
Through rubber soles you feel the pressure

Points where stones the size of a child's
Fist press through. How odd you look
When someone finds you there, your wife,
Your husband, the woman who cuts
Your hair—leaping from tarred tie to tie
Or over the dead hum of the third rail.
You circle some hole in the air, and sense,
Or seem to sense, a berth at last, some safe

Haven, fast passage, but you know better
Than that: No Silver Bullet where this line
Has been or bends, nothing but the crack
Of an old freight, its inhuman weight,
And the ride gone by, no one left behind
From whom to beg or barter a seat
But some clerk in a fin-de-siècle cap
Forever closing for the final time the gratitude

•

Of his grated window. Not even you can tell
If once that whistle blew steam in your
Electric childhood, or if that banked cry
Blooms now in your right or your wrong mind,
The wind-sway of weeds against your knees,
Pussy willow, burdock, no danger there,
Though in that absent blast, still in the blank
Flex of the horizon, you can't quite clear the track.

FIVE POEMS BY MO FEI

tr. Stephen Haven and Jin Zhong

Orchard

Touched by autumn
The orchard will become red and green
The fruit you pluck with your own hands is delicious
The bitter ones are still in the trees

If you throw a stone into the top of the tree
What falls is the completely red fruit
If your mouth meets an unpleasant taste
Certainly you have bitten the wrong place

After autumn
Snow will arrive
The fruit not collected in time
Will rot and drop like stones

Instant

The snow swiftly slides from the hilltop
The horse rolls on the ground
The shrubs cry in each other's arms
This instant

•

Is the longest year in memory
Unless the grandfather returns to light the lamp
No one dares finish reading
That fable glittering like fate

Facing a Stone

Facing a stone
My silence is nothing
A tree grows
Another tree also wants to grow
The branches entangled together
Have disturbed the leaf vein of a thought
What I want to say
What I do not want to say
Between them
There is a stretch of thick snow
The people who have fallen in love with winter
Leaving a deep track in the long road
Return on a full horse-cart with silver-white gallops

That Stone

That stone is overgrown with weeds
After the snow
It stirs the sunlight

•

That stone no longer beats
After death
It rests on the heart

That stone is an unknown spirit
After the snow
A gorge is formed in it

Falling Snow

Seeing the falling snow
I think of a person
A person who has never been to this county
She has never seen the winter here
Where the snowflakes flowing to the heart
Shine through the paper in the window
And she has never seen the snow-melting season
Where a still kite hangs on a wet jujube tree
Thinking of another falling snow
A snow which will not bury everything
I see another person:

She blooms in the dusk of that winter day
Her white descent is an experience
When she's lost
She reveals to me a pure territory
And on returning from that white day
I can't distinguish where it all ends:
The falling snow, that person

SHOOT

The white hair of their fine grip as soft as any newborn's,
They have survived their own germination, and my seeds':
Now the samara sprout in the garden too close
To my June house. What can they do but give themselves
To this sudden harvest? My daughter, five years from college,
Claws around me. I left my final snarl
In a horse-hair brush. Now only this wild, only
This bald reprieve: she brings it as she might a gift,
Her hands out before her, one shoot, its slight purchase
Of dirt. Cracked lifelines cup her offer. Whenever I read
What is written there, the mower cedes its right of way
To an oblong patch of longer grass, till the strung twig sways.

WATCH

Love like this never takes you by the wrist
Or against your absentmindedness
Alarms you with a quiet
More sure than its tick,

The point of origin
Some shop in Waltham, Mass.,
A twenty-five-year warranty
Etched on its one-hundred-year-old back.

Its slight weight
The absence of some wake,
The rosary of its turquoise beads
Marsupials, swallows out

Of the chimney's mouth.
Your grandfather's thumb
Has worn thin the one
Clasp that opens to the jewels

Of small things sprung. Far
From the satellite's web
Only through your touch it gains
Its quick again.

THREE POEMS BY DUO DUO

tr. Stephen Haven and Jin Zhong

It Is

It is   a shock of bright cloth
Along the horizon
Bleached by the rising sun
It is the moment day and night
Possess each other
It is twilight   a crippled face
Rising   breaking the metallic wall of night
      I love you
      I will never take back

It is   a hot tilting stove
The sun collapsing on the ridge
Loneliness rushes toward the abyss
It is the wind
A blind mailman   walks into the earth's depths
Its green blood
The erasure of all voices
My words go with him:
      I love you
      I will never take back

It is the song of the past   a string
Of small bells   their eyes staring
It is the clank of river shackles

Beating little drums
It is your eyes   two blue suns
Descending from the sky
        I love you
        I will never take back

It is two hammers   beating in turn
Forged in the fire of the same dream
It is the moon   heavy as a bullet
Riddling the water and the boat we sat in
It is mascara   sticking eternally
        I love you
        I will never take back

It is   lost
Swollen to a river
It is the flame of another flowing
The eternal hooks claw upward
It is the exact curve of fire
Shattering on star-shaped fingers
The fragments burning still   It is:
        I love you
        I will never take back

Longevity

Take the quiver of the heart in the bee's season gathering honey
Then the breath of the seeds then the opened eye
The spots on the dairy cow's back drift

Chasing the shadows of the sun
Oh the sun, originally, was the fruit of God
And his hand the gold basket for the fruit
The horse closes his contented eyelids
As if shoals of fish
Caught sight of the fisherman's beautiful face

Now is what it is: this summer
A train runs over and over
Breaks its own legs
The engineer walks in the fields
In the fields a watermelon steams heavily
Near scattered weeds and the sun's numerous nails
A flock of hens sell eggs in the light
The moon's faculae come typewritten in the sky
The horse takes off his mask, wholly made of bone
But now the dawn—who knows what it was waiting for—
Drowns all talk

The instructions come from the ancient breasts
And the seven pitchforks
From sleep and some hard food
In the pink brain of the horse
The sea surges into the window
The waves rot
The viscera of all things surrender
Because of their incapacity to feel shame
The tree sap trickles to a drip then stops
The tree withdraws its shadow from the field
Yesterday's chess match stalemates in a small station

The sown seed of memory roots
The universe narrows in the foxhunter's eyes
Yesterday's orange bleeds on his forehead
But He has heard their voices
Churning to a wet cement

One Story Contains All His Past

When he opens wide the windows all over his body toward the sea
And plunges to the clink of ten thousand knives
One story contains all his past
All the tongues plunge to this sound
And bring with them ten thousand knives
   which clink this sound
All the days crowd in one day
Then every year has one day too many

Last year falls right under the big oak
His memory comes from a cattle pen
A column of smoke rising from it
Some children, burning, sing hand in hand
   around a kitchen knife
Before dying out
The flames leap fiercely in the trees
The flames reaching so far as his scorched lungs

•

And his eyes are the festivals of two cities hostile to one another
The two pipes of his nostrils
Smolder with tobacco as they lift to the night
Women fire madly at his face with love
His lips are open for the deep kiss
In a moment, a train blasts past
Running in the opposite direction of death
His outstretched hands contain the morning
His hand pressing down the head of the sun

A silenced pistol declares the dawn
But the dawn's more desolate than breakfast's
Shattered plate on the floor
Where he waits on the funereal street
A fractured pendulum inaudibly keeps
The final time on an old door plank
One story contains all his past
The unnecessary palpitations of death

Fall as the stars fall, speeding toward Earth
The Earth looks for the snake's venom
So time rots outside its tick tick tock
On the rust stains of his copper coffin
Mice molt their teeth
Fungi stamp their feet on the putrid lichen
The sons of crickets hem his body permanently
And evil tears his face on a drum
Now his body fills with the glory of death
Fills with—one story contains all his past

•

One story contains all his past
For the first time the sun reads his near eyes
He rests, a long thin stick on a stump
A closer sun sits in his lap
Another burns between his fingers
Every night I aim at that one place
With a telescope till the sun dies out
A stump squats where that thin man sat

More silent than a cabbage bed in May
The horses he drives won't break their stride
In the early morning
Death shatters into a heap of glass
The thundering sun leads the veiled procession home
But the children's delicate feet
Step onto the eternal olive twigs
My head pounds, as if a thousand horse hoofs
Beat my drum
Compared with a thick crooked knife
Death's only a grain of sand
So one story contains all his past
And a thousand years turn their faces round—look

BEIJING STUDENT RIOT, MAY 12, 1999

Cold in a Beijing spring, an old man has gone four days without
       his insulin.
Even laser-guided missiles miss the mark? So says CNN,
Mistag the living for the dead. In an instant the Belgrade Chinese
       Embassy

Morphed to bric-a-brac and air, though dust motes still float.
Now, this morning, out on *An Jia Lou Lu*, the American Ambassador
Cannot go home. He barricades himself behind four tense marines:

Lucky for them they are monoglots and cannot even with
       pinyin placards
Speak their names. On the screen I try and cannot find
Students from *Beijing Shifan Daxue*. Somewhere they throw

Through an old man's window stones thousands of years old.
I am here, this morning, one year gone, in my rural Ohio home:
I'm glad they loved for a short while my daughter, my son.

And me? How often from that same American Embassy
I met their requests for the likes of *Casablanca, Mighty Aphrodite*,
Cueing my students into the joke when from deep space

Some Greek chorus summoned Zeus and America boomed
To the laugh of a prerecorded voice: *There is no one here to take
Your call right now: You know what to do: Please leave your prayer*

●

After the beep. I will get back to you. Politics is never personal.
So says Mario Puzo. My students didn't see
The Romantic in Bogart's Blaine: Even then, in 1942,

The propaganda of an American who thinks for everyone,
Never cracks a grin, smokes a Lucky Strike, drinks whiskey, gin,
And bends all Europe till the world is right. They asked for sex

And violence to stir their still nights. I gave them Brando, Pacino,
Talked it over awhile in a late-night *jiaozi* shop. One by one,
With *kuaizi* we lifted to our mouths fried kernels of salt.

They never slugged a beer, due deference to their foreign *laoshi*.
All the way to Shisha Pangma, the West thrusts its drilled insolence.
This morning I ask only for the counsel of Robert Duvall:

It's only business, after all, anonymous, strictly protocol,
Quiet in the way that it explodes
Always, from a distance, on someone somewhere known.

WINTER ARRIVES IN BEIJING, 1990

All October the old acrobat of autumn,
An ace slipped up its sleeve.
Then, suddenly, on a single day,
By tradition, by government decree,
The season unleashes one basic need:
The scent of cabbage, millions of heads.
We see them everywhere, on the backs
Of pick-ups, horse-drawn wagons.
The full measure of spring's
Hundreds of pounds of them.
So desire, so love is born of hunger.
Now we know what we'll eat
This January: Stacked like firewood
Along the *hutongs*, lining tiled roofs
And courtyards. Come winter,
Almost gray by then,
We'll wash the coal dust off of them.
But today the passion, the rush
To bring them in. As if it feared
To miss its chance, the season
Seizes the moment, and in an instant,
In passing, bears down on us.
We look up from our work, we go out
On the street to mark the quick of it:

One man spread-eagle on a load
Of cabbage, smiling back
As the traffic floats him past.
What's pressing, what's to come,
As if he knew our place among
The last long-shadowed warmth of the sun.

III

HEARTLAND

Now it makes sense the tactile pace that sudden tragedy takes,
How the mind cannot keep up with the body's avant garde,
The sensory charge of moments the changed self changes through
The way one catches the police car on the berm, then in the mirror,
Someone else's trouble flashing always everywhere behind you,
Then the sudden grit of it works its way down to your home
Like after the barber, before you shower, or else so thick
You feel the sudden stench of it, and wave your hands to no end,
Like in the house you once abandoned, though you took your kids.

What you remember are the flies, some Provencal of the mind
She always found each summer, where art was always free,
Swirling everywhere around her, dripping from the stars,
Though in the end she discovered ecstasy somewhere
Other than where she'd been, the anti-muse of her own kids,
Safe and distant, tucked in the Amish quilt
Of an American heartland. Still you heard the pulse of them
Through her cracked door, rushed the children back to the car,
Kept the engine idling, the A.C. on. Full of fear you went upstairs:

Who knows what might have come home early to roost there?
They massed in August like blackbirds on the desk you once built
For your daughter, on the drapes, the counters, your son's dresser.
Whatever gift the sun had given the earth in May doubled in spades.
You opened the house fully to that day, screened nothing out or in.
All it needed was a good airing. Then you found blood lines
Seeping from the freezer door, white fingers kneading black bread,
The outer appendages of some Rhapsody in White, some silent
Requiem for the dead. Full of self-righteous anger (you were always

•

Cleaning up after her), you gagged your way back to the car: *No problem,*
No Problem, you chanted to the children, and drove them home,
And never wanted to reach in, like some Doubting Thomas,
To touch that dead appliance. You gloved up, bagged and dragged
That mess to the road. Many years ago. But still it travels, more or less
Than personal. You catch it in the rear-view, flapping its one good wing
Or flashing behind you, the kids strapped in, or finally gone and grown,
The seeds of that old swarm crawling in you, on you, no matter where
You do not go, riding the shank of a mammal, right to your new home.

RUNNING LIGHTS

Caught in the terminal's long maw he watched
His lost flight blink backward from the gate.
Running lights they call them, wing tip and tail,
The pulse of the plane drawing without him
Toward the macadam's lift. Then in the distance,
Nothing but the glow of his long layover,
The city that took her from him, light years ago.

In the wake of that lost night, he imagines
The clustered rise of buildings, the steamed horizon
Like a giant mug of milk and tea, banked with snow.
Despite his long absence, no notice he called her,
Mumbled something about tomorrow's
Red-eye departure. *Oh, yes*, she whispered
On the phone, *oh yes* when he slipped a quarter

In a locker, half an hour after fumbled toward her.
She ran hot water, her warm sponge down his back.
Forever now, lion's paws and cracked porcelain
In the font of each kind act. He gathered the small
Destiny of that gesture, then her open wonder
When decades passed. Her loofah left small striations
Where he never scratched. Was it her mother told her,

•

Wash his back, he'll always remember?! He wonders if
She thinks her mother wrong in this, if she thinks
At all of that night's wick, flickering all day now
As he stares out a darker terminal, where each flight
Lacks a destination, where all connections lapse,
Each long-windowed corridor a Rhapsody in Black.
From where he sits, he slips again in her warm bath.

PICTURES AT AN EXHIBITION

Home from his daily primer my son's bent to prove
I couldn't possibly know who made up the rules:
He's sure there is a hierarchy of power
I have never thought of before. Like infinity
Minus one, he says. What's the answer
To that one? He says, *Dad, you don't know everything,*
And I agree, though that one's easy, that one's the mass

Of a dead body when Love does not present the eulogy.
Don't get carried away, Dad, he says, and knows
The score. Chess champ for his sixth grade, he plays
From memory Tcherepnin, Mussorgsky, Bach.
Then he tries me with another:
Who first said that letters should live inside
Of numbers, but never the other way around?

Sometimes it takes me all the time in the world
To figure out just exactly what he's talking about.
There's an *O* and an *N* and an *E* tucked
Inside the number *one*, but never a *1* in any name
Or word he knows of. I see, I say,
Though I don't really, and he slips out
The side door to the trampoline, where I catch him

•

Bobbing in and out of view of the kitchen window,
The order and randomness of his flips
Like quanta in the pressure of my nucleus.
Years ahead of his grade, unquantifiable,
Bullied from A-Z by a dominance
Of unknown variables, the new world order's
Nothing more than a complex pattern of X's

And O's, volatile as the fat molecules
Of some unstable gas, a wireless lexigraphy
Floating free, unseen until we touch its screen
In public spheres and in our own squares
Of warm domesticated air.
Relative to the rising laughter of my son,
The consonant that binds him back to earth again,

Caught as anyone in matter's downward pull
That pushes also each night upward
From the full simmer of the stove,
Taps on the pane of the kitchen, waves hello,
And in the mist that gathers there
Traces the name we share. It steams over,
Streaks the glass: nothing's new in that math.

LAND RUSH

Each evening my half-coon hound dog buries her snout
In her foul dish then comes up singing, moans, complains
About her condition, until I hook her up, let her shit
And piss among the graves—who's watching, anyway?—
The groundskeepers all home by then, their evening shows
Just flickering, the trees along the forested edge
Leaning as always toward distant centuries.
I mean no disrespect, consider myself half a naturalist,
Then like some homespun anthropologist
Who does not need to dig to question how his people live,

I hover over a watchtower that separates two graves:
Must have been Jehovah's Witnesses. Whenever I encounter
Their free subscription at my door, I ask them in,
Offer always a drink, all due respect
For my fellow citizens, certain that their strange belief
Gave Hitler no quarter. Now this one gives me succor:
Carpenter the last name, DAD: KING OF THE
REMOTE CONTROL at the tiled foot of the tombstone,
His favorite shows somewhere staying the channel.
Otherwise, this would not be paradise. Right next door,

The Cooks' black stone bowling ball, as if that's what
Their lives were for. Then in the alley
Between their graves, they've scored a spare,
Three fallen pins, another marker set next to them:

·

If tears could
Build a stairway
And Memories a lane
I would walk right up
To Heaven and bring
You home again

And here, in spades, a lover of cards, a chiseled Royal Flush,
The man lying for all eternity under the best possible draw
As long as the game is pure and there are no wild cards.
Some take their stand on their names only, and some
Are blank stone, and some burn batteries all night long,
Small running lights, carving a human space. O cracked globe,
O Saturn-like rings, O naked cupid sitting on a pole,
This father buried 1997, his wife born 1953 and counting,
A metal dragon fly, "Peace Be With You," shoved in his soil,
And next to him, no silence like this, his thirteen-year-old:

She once loved scarecrows, two on either side of her, sunflowers
No doubt plucked from some department store shelf
As if the girl's mother, unwilling, unschooled,
Walking among the dead, were forced to play
The Artist of the Beautiful, and lacking the tools
Turned to the Tiresias of some Walmart to drink our blood,
The bric-a-brac, the jingles we keep coming back to.
This is what he says when he speaks for us:
A planet, its orbit, another radiance in the ground, the curved
Wink of the moon, the young girl's dates burning in that circle.

SELF-PORTRAITS WITH AFRICAN CICHLIDS

1. *Documentary Photograph:*
   253 Guy Park Avenue, Amsterdam, New York

Beneath my chin the photographer sticks his lens.
What I know is this: the universe
Won't give it rest, this my hometown,
My native ground, this my first address.
Once in China, along a university *hutong*,
I saw two women play tennis without a net.
I thought of Frost, I thought,
All form breaks down. Then he asks
Me to grin. The holocaust of my mother's roses,
Everything that once begged something
Of her touch, hedges, poplars along
The side yard, apple, two cherry trees, rhubarb,
Now in blacktop (one doesn't need to mow
A parking lot), the backyard a lidless box,
Stars billowing from the top, the floorboards
Of both porches emulating new laws
For geometry, the photographer a good guy
From Jersey, packing it all in one frame.
There is a kind of fish that carries its own
Fry in the tongue-tie of its mouth.
I wonder what the word might be
For the moment they slip out utterly.

2. *Old Story*

Once I received, door to door delivery,
A card with this design: a man with a box
For a head, the river of heaven spilling out
The lid, the wife-drunk husband pounding
At the door, hammer in hand, mistaking me,
Though he had the right address,
For the sunken lover. My roommates and I
Could barely afford the rent. Someone is always
Screwing someone, someone's mad
In the refrain. *I'll bash your fucking head in,*
The wife's man said, some new ecstasy
Calming him from the form of his fury.
It is never quite enough to be on this Earth
Only one thing. A glass full to the brim,
Beyond the brim, and constantly emptying.
A hammer in hand and I asked him in!
What was I thinking? Let him use the phone.
No one home. I was twenty-two years old.
How's your hammer hanging, baby?
Heavy, heavy! There's no known species
That gives birth through its mouth.
These reasons to live alone.
I am fifty-three years old.

TASHTEGO DROWNING

The oiled perch of the main yard-arm is where you might see
The slippery edge of commerce and industry,
The decapitated head of all Nature hoisted, opened,

All humanity tapping, tapping to get in:
A single man held in the balance, with a sharp spade
Like a shaman on a board on a barrel

Calling his brothers to pray,
But high on a platform, above the ocean, searching out
The sweet spot, the momentary equilibrium

That keeps on shifting. As a man might bring
A woman to her full glass
That swells beyond the rim and only then

Spills the honey, this Wampanoag probing.
Then the hard edge of his bucket
Rammed down into the whale head,

Eighty, ninety gallons full, such a prodigious gift
Slid into tubs on deck, the colored clay
Of his home Aquinnah cliffs

Somewhere in the balance. Then something lets go,
Full immersion into that La Brea Tar Pit,
Like some human sacrifice, doomed fundamentalist:

•

A deep insuck of breath, wheeze of an asthmatic,
And in the flesh the gaping cranium animates
One last passing thought,

The life throb of a man, the world he knows,
Square knots, mizzen tops, tackles and blocks.
Then the ballasts slip, fizzing under water

Man, spent mammal, and lines that once held.
Tattooed Polynesian dives in, the crew urging him.
He bobs for a moment or two

Then gathers himself like a great warrior or orator
In some penultimate moment.
From the submerged dead, slit fountainhead

By the hair the obstetrician
Of that darker Asian draws the Aquinnah living
To the squeeze of the *Pequod*'s hands—

African, Persian, the blood brotherhood of one
Native son of Albany, who once called him honey.
This is Tashtego drowning.

THE LONGNOOK SEAL

for Bill Cohn, Charlotte Cohn, and Sue Dahl

That summer I was reading Henry Adams, the Gulf bled crude
That did not quite wash up in Louisiana bayous.
I tracked his mind forward and back in time. The gist of it
Did not rise. Adams thought the planet would survive
Only until 1925. Corporate robots burned
And cauterized the wound, and still an unheard hiss
Bubbled on my screen. A shaft disseminating what?
The underwater camera clarified nothing
But a constant hemorrhaging. An armada of absences
Couldn't brush the problem. I couldn't help but watch.
From my Provincetown studio, I directed my attention also
To a flower by Rousseau. Some reason of the eye
Kept Hopper there, and Homer, and for a while
The sculptor Paul Bowen. In 1862, twenty-four years old,
Adams thought the engine of Science
Soon beyond Man's control. The British tested
Armor piercing instruments, "The iron ships all utterly
Antiquated and useless." Coal heaped so high
He bet the race would soon commit suicide....
Then in 1907 he turned his attention to radium.
But this other Henri had half the Yucatan in mind,
Half the Parisian zoo: his lion kills
A water buffalo, so stylized the painting seems
More the idea of play than prey, and above them,
Right of the bananas, oleander, that all-seeing eye,
Deadly venom inside, the Gulf like a man who would not talk,
Ruined in deep thought. The flower by Rousseau a lovely portal.

•

All summer I touched the sullen Jeremiah of his thought,
His scowl from across the road on Pennsylvania Avenue,
Staring down each president as if each stole a world
Adams thought he owned. In his theory of degradation,
All things declined down some post-historic slide,
The profligate planet binging on some ooze
From Mesozoic forests, even human thought
"Vastly increased in apparent mass," "lost intensity
And continued to lose it with accelerated rapidity."
Black fields massing cold between each molecule
Like whole seas between our toes, everything pissing off
The old sun-stock. That was the fine rest
The future held for us. All things once moving
Barely quivering at -272 degrees C. So figured Adams,
Worse that a fucking Calvinist, brilliant despite
The seismic, anti-Semitic fault-line running through his life.
Railing against, advancing his own provincial track,
All perception but an eye, blue-blood loyal
To some native New England tradition, bit of a rebel in him,
Light stoking the mind's fire in its regard of matter.
I scanned his books online, via the Provincetown FAWC wi-fi.

It took old friends from Boston to scam me from that screen.
We walked along the harbor, drank ale, snapped lobster.
Up and down Commercial Street we found
The cathedral at Mont Saint-Michel, the Virgin Mary,
Poems, paintings, the Buddhist Goddess of Mercy,
"The one in a thousand of writers and artists,"
 "Fragments which flashed like jewels…"
While in a single pinch of dust the jolt to power

An entire city "would make in war short end of us."
For five bucks we bought glasses that masked us,
Warded off the sun with caps, sucked oysters that kept
For days a sea inside of us, and drove to the dunes
Where my parents once honeymooned. Adams,

Old Brahmin, I found you there, stunned in your late
Middle years, your hooded, sexless eye
Weaving in and out of time. After your wife's suicide,
You thrilled at the Shrine of Yeyasu,
Its carved and inlaid ceilings, its gilded pillars, flowers,
Mystic birds, and beyond it an entire Japanese village
Bathing naked! In the faux Zen garden
Every altar was tagged, summed to the dollar.
When we didn't listen too close, we pulled a note
Of beauty from the air, windless wind chimes,
Speakers hidden somewhere, clacking above
The thrum of the waterfall's electric pump
Like a loose-strung boat. For that was the province
Of the eye and not the ear, painters who had come
More than a hundred years, couples nuzzling each other
In affection or pure seminal power, blooming against
That other sense of weight, time, and sheared experience.

STILL LIFE

How easily the spirit worms its way into matter,
The perfect pitch, say, of this plum,
Curved and creased, throbbing with the slapped

Tincture of a newborn's cheeks, the on-call doctor
Already exhausted from his rounds,
The mother worn down from her dark labor,

The night nurse already worried about
Her husband's lover who will not speak
To her or anyone of her long years

As a single mother, and there it is again
Before the world screams in: Round
And round again, this California plum,

4040 USA about the size of a kid's
Thumbprint stickered on one side
To give it the FDA AOK.

It is one thing to regard from some slight
Distance the pith and pit of the matter,
Another to bite right in:

Sweet toothy pulp, yellow-green grin.
I spit the almond of its center, bits of flesh
Still stuck to it. No way it will survive

•

To blossom in some theatrical distance of sky
Beneath which there is no new Du Fu—
Not, anyway, in Ashland, Ohio—

Though if there were I would christen him
The manager of a landfill.
Packing his pipe, sweetening his tea,

Musing on the plum tree's wistful petals,
How gladly he receives
Each Monday's pick-up. What are the odds

For each single seed? So many poems
Of blossoms and plum trees!
Even the Son of Man sorrows on them:

Each morning he must eat one ripe fig,
Else he cannot shit. Oh, the sorry fate
Of each Romantic's a hemorrhoid or two:

Not even plums can help them
Though they wait in our markets
By the thousands, dyed to perfection,

Little Buddhas, tight little packages,
Waiting to fill a mouth.
If ever there were such a thing

·

As poetic justice, he said with aplomb.
Not one leaf. If I sat beneath
The blossoms of the plum tree I would stroke

The wisp of my long beard and strike a match. Not
In *this* state of things. Sweet cherry wafts
To 112th and Amsterdam. Rigor mortis

Of rush hour sets in. Once on my way
To where I once lived, the only motion
In the entire galaxy was some shared spasm

Involving a stranger and a baby, some cabbie
In the bottle-neck, the flash of my two-year-old
Glassed in, my daughter delighted by the sudden

Wheel of him. Light after light,
He rubbed his face with his hand. It matters
Nothing to me whether he was or was not

A good citizen. The fat day sang
Its usual hymn. The traffic burped and farted:
What does it take to make the dead man grin?

Before the teeth sink in,
Round and round and round
And round again.

THEY WERE DREAMING OF MANY THINGS

for Marina Epstein
Perry House Hotel, Bethlehem, New Hampshire, 1976

They were dreaming of many things they hadn't yet seen, Gorky,
      Nureyev,
Books they hadn't read, and once they carried with them
On a walk up Mt. Agassiz the long dead face in an Irishman's song
That hid itself behind a veil of stars. How else could he recall her,
In 30 years no word of her except in an old cracked photograph.

Now he remembers, beneath her nails, what she could never
Quite scrub out, flecks of paint, entire rainbows of them,
As if in touching him she pointed always toward some palette
Beyond where they sat naked on the rocks of the Ammonoosuc.
Then each evening they balanced silver trays, shoulder high, up on five

Fingertips, the chef named Sid throwing the rabbi out of the kitchen,
The rabbi who made his exodus from Egypt a few years before
The 1967 war, his full black beard hovering over what summered
On the cook's fat stove. Then the septuagenarians who came
Each August to simmer over their cold borsch heard all Brooklyn roar,

Even that far north, the Old Man in the Mountain a few miles away,
The hotel housing also Shorty, the dishwasher, the half-witted
Odd jobs man, who scrubbed one day with steel wool at his skin—
Smiling, showing everyone—see it takes the paint off—
Blood blotching up through the suds…. Then the baker—Mr. Bailey—

•

Straight from Harlem—never heard of challah, the sweet rise of it
The bane of him: They took advantage when Mrs. Perry fired him,
Squatters' rights to the baker's private bedroom, she a shikseh,
Half Jewish only, since everyone there was counting,
And he the Shabbat goy, an Anglican who wore a yarmulke
      to fit right in.

It seemed, even then, a good thing, a love more remembered than lived,
And some lapsed wisdom they almost took in hand,
How they never even feared their own ignorance
Or knowledge that was sure to come in large and small parts
Always to scar them. All around them dark men gathered
      on dark porches

In the pulse of ancient song. They offered them no entry, no invitation,
So they listened anyway, murmured not one word slow nights long.
Never did they lift one sweet glass of wine to that nocturnal thrum,
Or break bitter herbs, salt unleavened bread, still she remembered
What she heard, once at Taizé, when the monks sang:

Joy seasoning sorrow, sorrow joy. Long afternoons
They watched in deep clear pools trout hardly quivering,
Moving so they would not move. Mouths against the current,
They barely felt September's pull, whole bodies holding
Their own in the drift, taut in the stream, stock-still.

ON THE ONE HAND

I remember, now, a television show I didn't much like
But as a boy watched anyway, some slap-stick comedy
Of a haunted house in which a single hand appeared,
Popping up like a Jack-in-the-Box out of a trap door
In the floor or from some tabletop.
It sewed with its white glove some laughable meaning

To silence. With its pointer finger, with the flat of its palm,
It stopped the unexpected visitor dead in his tracks.
Laughter can do that. It gave the AOK, or the No Way
José, or rolled up like a hedgehog, or wavered in
Palm-down indecision. Within the range of what a single
Hand might say, it thumbed the audience in

And never once that I can remember tried to hitch a ride.

~

In the portrait of the surgeon Clarence Moore,
As if Diego Rivera understood the essence
Of an office, how in the rough and slick
Of a man's palm it floats
Faceless among us, the emery board
Of the carpenter's, the poet's soft white

•

Turtles absent of their shells,
There is little else of Dr. Moore
In the composition but his white scrubs
And one hand holding a scalpel
To the half-severed limb of a tree
In the form of the human body.

The other hand—for Rivera the other hand
Was always the beauty and difficulty
Of the matter—dabs away sap
While the roots go down and the atoms
Of known elements balance like baubles
In the upper branches. But this is the story

~

Of the single hand: a few days after the funeral,
One emerged on a fast-food arterial
That sprung up in the '50s like some strange
American Beauty and stayed with us ever since.
From the window of a *Firebird*, in the drive-thru,
It gripped the white bag of salt and oil, then pulled

Onto the sizzle of the arterial and I followed.
I forgot for the moment the life attached to it
(The tail of its white sleeve streaming after it),
As if it were its own entity, as if, in the same lane,
Lagging one car behind, I might receive from it
Some sign, something more than *Hurry up*

•

And turn already, more than the flipped bird.
Before we finally drifted off on the separate
Arcs of our exits, it flicked off ashes
Then shot the cherry back. Small stars scattered
Across the blacktop. Out on its own the hand
Opened and closed like some sea anemone

Suspended in the gentlest of waves.
Then it thrummed to nothing I could hear,
No Classic Rock drifting back, as if in some
Silent choreography. It was not
My father's hand—all that is left of it....

~

I have seen them in Rivera's *Detroit Industry*
Complete with the witches of all cardinal points,
The Captains of Foundries, the Goodness
Of the North, a parallel arc of bodies and gears
Spooning each other in some mythic
New World Harmony

Only Luther or Lenin could scheme up.
Around them the isolation of human fists
Ripping minerals out of the dirt
Like severed heads planted in some garden
Of the *Night of the Living Dead.*

•

It was not the sound of one hand clapping
Or the hand you take in marriage,
Not the conductor holding the still power
Of Brahms one moment longer
In the whorls of a fingertip.

It was not the yarmulke of the human hand
That presses us back to earth again,
Nor the hand that bids the children wait
While all the universe weighs in
For the altered touch of the priest.

It was the left hand I saw there, always now the left,
Neither waving goodbye nor hello. Not Phaeton
In the wreck of it, not his father's daily diligence
Signaling in the mouth of the exit.
Not keeping time, not even keeping the measure

Of where we are, *Taurus, Nova, Subaru, Pulsar,*
And this one a *Firebird,* speeding without purpose
In the pulse of the current, floating on air
For the sheer joy of it. Above the tick, the blur
Of cracked tar, one hand free, strapped to a star.

LAST LIGHT

Though the sun has clearly set now on Inness and his vision
There is, in *Summer Landscape, 1894*, something of paradise
Thomas Jefferson dreamed of all his life, one dark figure,
Another lighter beyond him, the eye more fully drawn
To the mind of the darker, leaning slightly into the turn
Of the grass's low horizon, the lift of three nearby trees,
Limbs trimmed so herds might better graze near them,
Rising with the gesture of the mind to the light sky-haze.

Everything's smeared with this one view: early September,
Late afternoon, the magenta of Man at home in his world.
Cattle fade in the gloam, no wild ass of a man, no hand ever
Raised against them. The peace that passes understanding
Throttles in a songbird's throat. Toward the further horizon,
Three chords of color lighten finally to the speckled blue
And white of sky: dark bottom band, then blue-green grass,
Then the far field, distant trees, ceding to autumn and its tones.

The central man is all these things, parallels the lift of trees,
But dark like the foreground bovine that nearly dissolves
Into the black, the night-green crosshatch of grass.
Three elms mushroom but not toward our own century.
Nothing he could ever spirit tethered there, almost free.
Diminished by distance, his nearby plot nowhere imminent
Or the one war he knew, nowhere that long year's tracks
Buried in stone, bloom of coke and steel, lost wages, lost bread,

•

The Pullman Boycott dead murmuring in the lien
Of some lapsed wilderness, New Jersey and its continent.
Where is Eugene Debs in the light of this last lyric?
No sign of rain, though still in the dark swath something takes
To ground, the black tilt of the mind, this rogue lush calm
Cohering, collapsing, imagined into being, till we know
That this is in us, necessary, superfluous, bearing through some
Wild dream, the Garden as it never was, and never again will be.

TANK

When you died the universe spread out more fully

The dog in its fenced-in yard barked

As always we took him for a walk

Hundreds sang your absence too

It was not that way with the rest of the world

One dagger, one feather from the past

Urned its message in

Everything the Earth can never change

In the interstellar stole of space

In the surplice of the sky

I grieved and the grass refused to grieve with me

The trees along the walk were the same

The dog shat and pissed as always

One neighbor complained

•

My right arm yanked in the exact direction

A squirrel scuttled away

From the thump of an approaching car

The car from the spark of a train

In my muzzle of air, the white stitch of the sky

Bellying by

Deep sea divers, all of us

The dog's name was Barnabus

ACKNOWLEDGMENTS

Thanks are due to the editors of the following publications, in whose pages some of the poems in this book first appeared:

American Poetry Review: "Orchard"; "That Stone"; "Facing a Stone"; "Instant"; "Falling Snow" (Mo Fei poems translated by Stephen Haven and Jin Zhong); "It Is"; "Longevity"; "One Story Contains All His Past" (Duo Duo poems translated by Stephen Haven and Jin Zhong)

Artful Dodge: "In the Street" (a Mang Ke poem translated by Stephen Haven and Wang Shouyi)

Asheville Poetry Review: "Heartland"; "They Were Dreaming of Many Things"

The Common: "Land Rush"; "The Longnook Seal"

Consequence Magazine: "Minute Man"; "Shelter"; "Beijing Student Riot, May 12, 1999"

Guernica: "Fu Han at the Nuts Café, Chongqing, China, April 9, 2011"

5 a.m.: "Splashdown: Apollo 13"

Image: "Blood Blessing"; "Stole"

Key Satch(el): "Winter Arrives in Beijing" (in earlier version)

Parnassus: "The Last Sacred Place in North America"

Poetry Miscellany: "People Age Even After Death" (a Mang Ke poem translated by Stephen Haven and Wang Shouyi)

Poetry New Zealand: "Self-Portraits with African Cichlids," "Room in a Room," "Watch"

Northwest Review: "Talisman"; "The Last Train By"

The Southern Review: "Pictures at an Exhibition"

All five translations from Mo Fei's poetry, Mang Ke's "In the Street" and "People Age Even After Death," and all three translations from Duo Duo's poetry, were reprinted in *The Enemy in Defensive Positions: Poems from China* (Poetry Miscellany Chapbooks, University of Tennessee—Chattanooga, 2008).

Thanks to the Ohio Arts Council, the Fulbright Foundation, the MacDowell Arts Colony, the Yaddo Foundation, and the Provincetown Fine Arts Work Center for grants and residencies that supported the writing of these poems.

Finally, thanks to Michael Miller—fine poet and friend—for his repeated readings of these poems. Many thanks also to Eric Pankey.

STEPHEN HAVEN is the author of two previous collections of poetry, *Dust and Bread* (Turning Point, 2008), for which he was named 2009 Ohio Poet of the Year, and *The Long Silence of the Mohawk Carpet Smokestacks* (University of New Mexico/West End Press, 2004). He is also author of the memoir *The River Lock: One Boy's Life Along the Mohawk* (Syracuse University Press, 2008). His poems have appeared in *The Southern Review*, *American Poetry Review*, *Parnassus*, *Salmagundi*, *Northwest Review*, *Image*, *Western Humanities Review*, *World Literature* (Beijing), and in many other journals. He is Director of the Ashland University MFA Program in Poetry and Creative Nonfiction in Ashland, Ohio, and Director of the Ashland Poetry Press.